Meet Pat the Penguin

By Sophie Reese   **Illustrated by Jackie Snider**

Target Skill Consonant Pp/p/

Scott Foresman
is an imprint of

penguin

I am Pat the penguin.

painter

 I am a little painter.

popcorn

I like to have popcorn.

I am Pat the penguin.